Deserts

If you landed here, you might think that you were on the moon or Mars!

But it is not the moon or Mars! It is a desert on our planet.

What is a desert? A desert
is land that gets little rain.
A desert gets less than
25 cm of rain in a year!

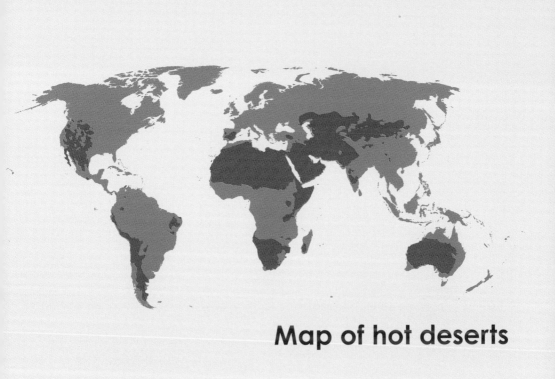

Map of hot deserts

A lot of the land on our planet is desert. All seven continents have them. The brown parts on the map are deserts.

We think of a desert as
being hot, but some
deserts are freezing!

Some deserts are hot when it is bright, but freezing in the night. Some deserts are flat. Some have steep hills of sand.

Arctic desert

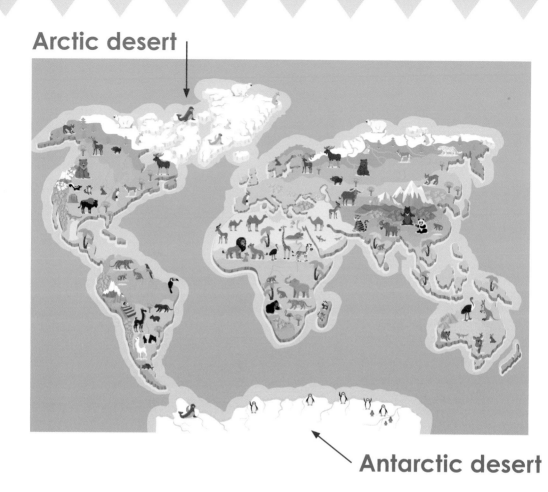

Antarctic desert

The biggest desert on our
planet is the Antarctic
desert. It is freezing.

The next biggest desert is
the Arctic desert and that
is a freezing one too!

Living in a desert is hard
with the lack of rain.

But some living things have adapted well to living there, like this horned lizard.

Look at all the living things that can exist in a desert with so little moisture.

You might see a cactus bursting up from the sand.

This is a desert bighorn sheep.

Camels fit well into a desert.
They can go for a week or
longer without a drink.

This desert cottontail
rabbit gets its food and
drink from a cactus.

Deserts are interesting parts of our planet. But do not mix them up with desserts!

Words to blend

landed	planet	land
continents	flat	sand
biggest	next	exist
drink	adapted	cactus
bighorn	longer	rabbit
Arctic	Antarctic	seven
camels	rain	year

Before reading

Synopsis: What is a desert? Is it always hot? Can it be cold too?

Review graphemes/phonemes: ee oi ow ur igh

Book discussion: Look at the cover and read the title together. Ask: *What kind of place is a desert? What do you think we will find out in this book?*

Link to prior learning: Display a word with adjacent consonants from the book, e.g. *freezing*. Ask children to put a dot under each single-letter grapheme (f, r, z, i) and a line under the digraphs (*ee, ng*). Model, if necessary, how to sound out and blend the sounds together to read the word. Repeat with another word from the story, e.g. *brown*, and encourage children to sound out and blend the word independently.

Vocabulary check: adapted – adjust to changes over a period of time

Decoding practice: Write these words on cards: *bursting, bright, moisture, steep*. Hold up one card at a time for children to read. Encourage fluent reading on sight, without overt sounding out and blending, as far as possible.

Tricky word practice: Display the word *there* and ask children to circle the tricky part of the word (*ere*, which makes the /air/ sound). Practise writing and reading this word.

After reading

Apply learning: Ask: *Which part of this book did you find most interesting? Would you like to visit a desert one day? Why, or why not?*

Comprehension

- Can you name a freezing desert?
- Can you name an animal that is well-adapted to living in the desert?
- Why might you muddle up deserts and desserts?

Fluency

- Pick a page that most of the group read quite easily. Ask them to reread it with pace and expression. Model how to do this if necessary.
- Children could choose a favourite page to read aloud. Can they make their reading sound natural and fluent?
- Practise reading the words on page 17.

Tricky words review

our	were	there
being	some	here
one	like	all
they	into	so
do	you	the